catastrophe in indonesia

MAX LANE

LONDON NEW YORK CALCUTTA

Seagull Books 2010

© Max Lane 2010

ISBN-13   978 1 9064 9 767 5

British Library Cataloguing-in-Publication Data
A catalogue record for this book is available
from the British Library

Jacket and book designed by Sunandini Banerjee, Seagull Books
Printed at Graphic Print, Calcutta, India

THE CRASH OF THE LEFT IN 1965

Rarely has any modern country been through a political experience that has completely and utterly reversed its direction and redefined and turned inside out its culture. This is what happened in Indonesia during the decade or more that began with one of the most devastating state-managed campaigns of murder and terror in the twentieth century.

The massacre of more than a million Indonesians between October 1965 and 1967[1] remains one of the most effective and gruesome campaigns of terror in recent times. Over a period of approximately two years, hundreds of thousands were murdered—often to maximize the terror effect—in a variety of ways that included beheadings, disembowellings and en masse machine-gun executions in prison cells. People were taken away at night, then shot and buried.[2] The targets: anyone sympathetic to President Sukarno or to the political parties or groups that supported him, the most significant of which were the Indonesian Communist Party (Partai Komunis Indonesia, PKI)[3] and its affiliated mass organizations, and the Indonesian National Party (Partai Nasional Indonesia, PNI).[4] Smaller leftist groups, like the Trotskyist Young Communist Force (Angkatan Comunis Muda, ACOMA) or the independent revolutionary nationalist Indonesian Party (Partai Indonesia, PARTINDO), were not spared either.

Thousands of Indonesians escaped being murdered only to find themselves imprisoned. The number of detainees between 1965 and 1967 is unknown but at least 20,000 people were kept in prison camps, without trial, until 1979. Only a handful were ever brought before the military's kangaroo courts.

While Sukarno's supporters formed the targets of the massacre, its agent was the Indonesian Army, itself purged of all pro-Sukarno men. The Army, assisted by anti-communist militia groups—sometimes nationalist, sometimes Muslim—and under the leadership of General Suharto, was the main instrument of terror.

The massacre succeeded in, literally, reversing the direction of Indonesian history. The radical Left in Indonesia, led by a complicated axis between President Sukarno and the PKI, had organized, by 1965, at least 20 million people across various parties and mass organizations. The Sukarno–PKI alliance enjoyed great popular support and seemed—at least, from the point of view of the people—poised for a seizure of power until the reign of terror launched by Suharto on 1 October 1965.

The massacres were followed by rapid steps to consolidate the political victory of the counter-revolutionary terror. The PKI and other leftist organizations were banned, along with their publications as were those of all left-wing writers. The 'spreading of Marxism Leninism' was forbidden, and trade unions and other popular organizations disappeared altogether for at least the next seven years. Those that later reappeared were reduced to no more than extensions of the state apparatus.[5] This consolidation was further strengthened by a complete rewriting of Indonesian history, a project implemented by the History Centre of the Indonesian Armed Forces which depicted all mobilizations of the popular classes as evil or disruptive, the PKI and the Left as anti-national and the Army and military figures as the only consistent strand of good in Indonesian history. This new history was taught across the country, from primary schools to universities. The elimination of so many leftists and the physical terror, alongside the banning of organizations and publications, meant that there was no alternative viewpoint—not even from the margins—for the next 33 years, until the fall of Suharto in 1998.[6]

A new Indonesia was thus created in Suharto's image: corrupt, repressive and dependent in almost all respects on the 'West'.

How could such a hugely popular President and such a rapidly growing organized Left be so completely annihilated? Many left-wing movements have suffered repression, but none so effectively total as the Sukarno–PKI alliance. The PKI tried to launch a guerrilla regroupment in Java in 1968 but was again repressed by the military. Since then, despite fragments of the PKI existing underground, there has been no meaningful attempt at a rebuilding. Not only was the movement crushed but Indonesia itself was forced to abandon its revolutionary past. Its national literature, the most important embodiment of both the rebellion against tradition and the articulation of radical and liberating visions of the future, was no longer taught to its young. Several generations have now been educated in a drastically falsified version of their history and have had no access to their greatest treasure—their nation's literature.

According to Pramoedya Ananta Toer, Indonesia's leading novelist, 'Suharto and his regime lacked any sort of idealism. That's why our culture degenerated into trivia and entertainment, and eventually became so shallow that a normal human brain could find nothing to digest.'[7]

How did this catastrophic transformation—from a society where 20 million people were mobilized in radical politics to one where 'a normal brain could find nothing to digest'—take place?

OPPORTUNITY AND PRETEXT

The first part of the answer must relate how the opportunity arose and what the pretext was for Suharto and the Army to unleash an era of systematic and violent purges. Both were provided by the abortive mutiny-turned-coup organized by D. N. Aidit, Chairperson of the PKI, and his Special Bureau,[8] on the evening of 30 September and the morning of 1 October 1965. This action, which involved mobilizing pro-Sukarno and pro-PKI parts of the Armed Forces so that they would detain anti-PKI military leaders, was organized without any discussion with the rest of the PKI leadership. Secrecy, after all, is a fundamental feature of midnight conspiracies.

Aidit's Special Bureau, headed by Kamaruzaman (known as Sjam), organized the soldiers of the Presidential Guard to visit the homes of key generals in the High Command who were then to be detained. The plan was to later present them before Sukarno and to convince him that they were plotting against him and that they thus needed to be replaced.[9] As soon as this was done, a newly formed Revolutionary Council would send out the call for more such councils to be formed throughout the country in order to lead the campaign for the ousting of all right-wing officers. However, the conspiracy was doomed from the start. Some generals were killed as was an officer and a young daughter of one of the generals. In the end it was the conspirators,

instead of the detained generals, who found themselves before the President, trying to explain the
night's events.

Sukarno, learning of the situation, immediately
brought the operation to a halt, thus completely
puncturing Aidit's conspiracy. What made things
worse was that, in the consequent chaos, the detained generals were assassinated anyway. Once
Sukarno regained control of his Presidential Guard,
Aidit found himself in a corner and faced with
imminent disaster. Refusing to back down, he
ordered the Special Bureau to continue with the
plan. A decree (Decree No. 1) was broadcast over
the national radio—already under the control of the
conspirators—in the early afternoon which declared
Sukarno's Cabinet decommissioned.[10] The conspiracy thus swiftly escalated from a mutiny hoping to
win Sukarno's support to a coup against Sukarno
himself. It was, however, too late. Sukarno's inability
to support a midnight conspiracy of extra-judicial
killings combined with the escalation from mutiny
to coup, with the clear involvement of elements from

the PKI leadership, provided the Army with both the opportunity and pretext to seize the political initiative.

Moreover, General Suharto, head of the Army Strategic Reserve Command (Komando Cadangan Strategis Angkatan Darat, KOSTRAD) which commanded all these forces, had been informed of the impending mutiny by some of the conspirators who had imagined him to be either supportive of or neutral about Sukarno and the PKI. Suharto watched and waited. As soon as the conspiracy was revealed, he declared his opposition to the 30 September Movement, condemned the killings and accused the PKI of being responsible. He seized effective control of the Armed Forces and took a series of steps over the coming weeks which both isolated Sukarno and gave him total power over Indonesia. And then the killings began.

But are these events really part of the answer? Are we not, in fact, faced with even more questions? How and why did Aidit plot such a midnight conspiracy with the Presidential Guard when the

Sukarno–PKI alliance already had millions of supporters? Was it part of PKI strategy? Neither question delves into the heart of the matter. Both the PKI and Sukarno were, in fact, mired in a mass of contradictions inherent in the social landscape of Indonesia, contradictions further intensified by some of the PKI's tactical decisions which were in complete contrast to its fundamental strategic outlook.

INDONESIA'S UNIQUE POLITICAL LANDSCAPE

The rapid growth of the PKI and radical Sukarnoism was partly due to the uniquely weak ideological hegemony of what masqueraded as a ruling class in independent Indonesia. If, accepting Karl Marx's dictum that the ruling ideology is always the ideology of the ruling class, we ask the question: Who and what was the Indonesian ruling class in the 1950s and 60s?—then the uniqueness of Indonesia's political landscape will be quickly revealed.

Indonesia, at the time of its independence (declared by Sukarno in 1945 and formally acknowledged by the Dutch in 1949), was a capitalist society.

The economic system was based on the private ownership of productive property, including land. The state, the Army and civil service, was in the hands of the class of property owners. Workers, landless labourers and the huge sea of pauperized petty owners were yet to become organized enough to challenge this power. The PKI began to grow only after 1952 and President Sukarno began to re-profile his leftism only after 1957.

But what about the Indonesian bourgeoisie? It was a weak, under-resourced, stunted and fractured class, with little political organization, almost no national cultural development and no social weight except as a local parochial elite. A consequence no doubt of three centuries of colonial rule.

It was, in fact, the Netherlands bourgeoisie which dominated the political and economic life of the Malay Archipelago (excluding the Malay peninsula) for more than 300 years, starting from the sixteenth century, through systems of indirect rule, subjugating and deploying as tools the various hereditary rulers—rajas, sultans and others—in various parts of the country. Even in the nineteenth and twentieth centuries, when the Dutch imposed a more systematic administrative and political structure in the region, the Netherlands Indies government continued to make use, wherever possible, of the remnants of traditional rule.

One consequence of this centuries'-long colonial humiliation and oppression of the archipelago's local despotic classes was the utter destruction of their political authority. Indonesian society was only marginally modernized—the Dutch did not develop anything more than a colonial economy. As a result, many pre-bourgeois, traditional, cultural values managed to survive even as the overall structures of despotic ideology and authority were destroyed. The foreign colonial state ruled, for all intents and purposes, as a dictatorship and stamped out any signs of the development of a well-resourced, property-owning class. All the most productive agricultural and mineral resources were in Dutch or other European hands; the same applied for the large-scale international and colony-wide trade. And most medium- and small-level wholesale and retail trade was channelled into migrant Chinese hands.

As Sukarno summed up in a comparison between Indonesia and India in the 1920s, the economic world of the Indonesians was 'a society branded with the mark of the small'.[11] Land ownership consisted mainly of tiny plots; entrepreneurs had tiny amounts of capital and supplied tiny local markets; and workers and coolies earned miserably small wages. Today there remains only small trading, small shipping, small farming and millions of workers who own nothing at all.

It was this highly localized, parochial, small-scale, under-resourced domestic bourgeoisie—not yet even a national bourgeoisie, serving a national market and with a national perspective—which inherited the state from the Dutch in 1949. And all of the political parties, except the PKI, were dominated by elements drawn from this class. Not surprising, then, that support for each of these parties, despite their attempts to develop as national organizations, was concentrated in specific parts of the country.

Therefore, when she threw off the shackles of colonialism and emerged as a new state, Indonesia had neither a hereditary despotic class nor a national bourgeoisie that could consolidate state power. Nor did she have the cultural or ideological resources to rapidly establish the hegemony of bourgeois ideology—of the right of property-holders to grow rich or of the idea that citizens should remain atomized voters in occasional elections. In fact, the struggle against colonialism, led mainly by radicalized intellectuals and based on the mobilization of the masses, had created a new, if still-developing, hegemony— that of struggle, activity and social justice. After independence, this axis between the radicalized intellectuals and the mobilized masses stood in immediate contradiction to the parties of the domestic, not-yet-national, bourgeoisie.

RAPID RADICALIZATION OF THE MASSES AND
RAPID MILITARIZATION OF THE BOURGEOISIE

This particular post-independence axis received a boost from the Japanese occupation of Indonesia during 1942–45. The occupiers promised rapid independence for Indonesia (within the Asian Co-Prosperity Sphere) and allowed pro-independence leaders, including Sukarno, to travel the country and speak at public meetings about Indonesian independence being part of Japan's strategy to win support for its war effort. In the face of worsening oppression and exploitation under the Japanese, however, the latter goal was not achieved but Sukarno was able to consolidate the commitment to independence as well as his relationship with the masses. Given their limited number of experts in Indonesian language and culture, Sukarno was also often able to talk past his Japanese escorts.

As soon as it was clear that a Japanese defeat in the war was imminent and that there was no longer going to be any effective state apparatus of repressions, elements from all classes of Indonesian society began to organize themselves into radical groups. The PKI itself was re-established in October 1945, after being suppressed and disbanded by the Dutch in 1927. A ferment of radicalism spread through the country with the formation of different socialist and communist, labour and peasant groups and it was on them that Sukarno found himself relying while he tried to create a new state power—one that could successfully combat the well-equipped and efficient Dutch capitalist class (who quickly sent back an army to take back their colony)—in the vacuum left by the departing Japanese. Despite his attempts at consolidating power in the larger national interest, some of the groups—such as those led by Tan Malaka, a maverick communist, separated from the PKI—tried to wrest leadership from him and the other Left groups, one of them even going so far as to kidnap the prime minister.

It is hard to be clear about the size of the organizations due to the chaotic nature of the times and the minimal documentary evidence, but it is clear that the number of armed Leftist groups grew in tandem with their political influence. Post-1945 was also the only period when PKI members and other communists functioned as working members of the Cabinet. By the 1960s, Aidit and one other senior PKI leader were part of the Cabinet only by dint of their position as deputy speakers of the House of Representatives. No PKI leader has headed any significant ministry in the Indonesian Cabinet since the 1940s. The PKI and other leftist seats in the early Cabinets were obtained primarily through Sukarno's mediation.

Anti-communist civilian political forces, in keeping with the clear evidence of the Left's influence and Sukarno's own proximity to it, quickly became dependent on anti-communist military forces for their defence. Urged by a visiting delegation from the United States, the right wing of the Indonesian Cabinet, especially Prime Minister Mohammad Hatta, ordered those sections of the Army under anti-communist leadership to disarm and demobilize the armed Left. Innumerable clashes took place between the Army's forces and left-wing guerrilla groups between 1947 and 1948, culminating in a major encounter between Hatta's Army and PKI forces in Madiun, East Java.[12] The PKI seized the city and tried to make it a base for the formation of a new radical government, one it hoped Sukarno would support. However, the PKI, and the Left in general, was far from ready to establish a national government, especially in the face of the yet-unfinished struggle against the returning Dutch. Sukarno went on the radio and gave the masses an ultimatum—support him or support Musso, then PKI chairperson. In the meantime, the Army came down heavily on all PKI forces. PKI leaders were arrested; according to some versions, several were later executed on the orders of Hatta, despite Sukarno's visible opposition to such acts.[13] Some of the excesses of the PKI forces were also used as a pretext to kill thousands of its members and supporters.

The history of the Left, of the PKI and of the relationship between Sukarno and the Left during the 1945–49 period of war against the Dutch is complicated and remains disputed. It is not the aim of this essay to delve into this period in detail but to make one important, indeed central, point—the Indonesian Army, as it emerged in the 1940s and as it was consolidated later, *was ready to carry out a large-scale massacre of the Left*. This was the crucial lesson learnt at Madiun and it was a lesson that the Left would never forget. While both sides perpetrated violence in the aftermath of the Madiun fiasco, it was the government under the right-wing prime minister, Hatta, which consciously organized the arrests and executions of political leaders, all of whom belonged to the Left. Sukarno, trying to maintain a semblance of unity in his government while faced with military attacks from the Dutch, often found himself losing the initiative to Hatta.

Indeed, the next decade reveals an abundance of evidence regarding the violent and reactionary nature of the Indonesian Army.

1951: The Army claims a coup in the offing and arrests 2,000 PKI members. Detained for several months, they are released without trial.

1952: The Army, having demobilized almost all guerrilla groups, surrounds the Presidential palace with canons and demands that Sukarno dismiss the government. Sukarno refuses and finally succeeds in talking down the rebellion.

1956–57: Right-wing elements in the Army seize control of several provinces and arrest trade unionists and leftists.[14] These groups later form the Provisional Revolutionary Republic of Indonesia (Pemerintah Revolusioner Republik Indonesia, PRRI), supported by the most anti-communist of political parties, the Council of Indonesian Muslim Associations (Majelis Syuro Muslimin Indonesia, MASYUMI)[15] and the pro-Western Indonesian Socialist Party (Partai Sosialis Indonesia, PSI).[16] The Army right wing receives direct military support from the United States but splits over this rebellion which is ultimately suppressed by forces loyal to the legal government. However, the establishment of prison camps and the arrest of the Left once again indicates the willingness of the Army to deploy repressive violence.

1956–65: Seven assassination attempts are made on Sukarno's life, including one grenade attack and two aircraft bombings of his home. The Army is found responsible for all of them.

This historical trend meant that, from 1948 onwards, the spectre of a military coup, of Army massacres and imprisonments, continued to haunt the Left, including Sukarno. The rapidly growing left-wing mass movement ideologically led by Sukarno, especially after 1959, and (mainly) organized by the PKI, was an unarmed political presence under constant threat of repression and massacre. When, after 1960, the movement's growth witnessed a rapid acceleration, its central crisis continued to be the formulation of a method for dealing with the threat of the hostile Armed Forces.

The flip side of a weak bourgeois ideological hegemony was that the Army could so easily embark on a series of massacres against the leftists so early in the new republic's history. Only violent repression, it seemed, could stem the tide of radicalism.

In 1949, within a few years of the establishment of a non-violent political order—parliamentary democracy rather than revolutionary republic—the PKI experienced a revival followed by a rapid growth and, within a decade, Sukarno was able to seize the political initiative from his conservative opponents.

By 1952, therefore, a new leadership had established itself, headed by D. N. Aidit. By the time of the 1955 general elections, the PKI had emerged as one of the four principal parties, winning 16.4 per cent of the ballot (6,176,914 votes).[17] When provincial elections were held in 1957, the numbers increased, with the poor masses of Java forming the largest body of support. This steady growth continued into the 1960s as the PKI allied itself with Sukarno's campaign (begun in the 1950s) to recover West Papua from Dutch hands, to nationalize Dutch and other foreign interests, to institute some form of land reform and to block the formation of Malaysia from occurring without a referendum in Sabah and Sarawak. By 1963, the PKI was claiming that, along with its mass organizations, it had a membership of over 20 million. A number perhaps not very far from the truth.[18]

The same decade which saw PKI membership grow from a few thousand to nearly 20 million also witnessed the growth and radicalization of another party, the PNI. By 1965, it too was several million strong and had successfully expelled its right-wing and anti-communist leaders. Clearly, this movement, which had the support of the President, could only be stopped from assuming power—and there was no doubt that a Sukarno–PKI alliance would have won any elections held after 1960—by the Army.

CONTRADICTIONS IN TACTICS

This rapid growth of radical mass movements—and hence the popularity of the PKI, the PNI and Sukarno—was possible due to the weaknesses of the domestic bourgeoisie. But this social class, despite its apparent flaws, always wanted to develop an army that was able and willing to repress these new and radical forces. A confrontation between the Left and the Armed Forces therefore seemed inevitable. The question was: When and how would it take place?

The answer to this question may perhaps also answer another: What was the mechanism or process which would allow the Left to come to power, given the Army's violent hostility?

The political context or framework within which these questions began to be more concretely posed was created by the launch of what Sukarno called Guided Democracy, a new political arrangement begun in 1959.

Guided Democracy

Guided Democracy was formally based on a Presidential decree which reinstituted the emergency constitution under which the Republic functioned between 1945 and 1949. A generally democratic document, it guaranteed basic rights and a prime minister and a Cabinet appointed by the president. However, its emergency nature meant that it was brief and provided scant details for the establishment of a system of government. Sukarno decreed the 1945 Constitution into force on 5 July 1959,[19] the pretext being the inability of a Constituent Assembly—elected in 1955—to arrive at a two-thirds' majority agreement on a new constitution even after three years of discussions. Although Sukarno could have continued with the Constitution that had been in force since 1950, there was another reason underpinning his move—the hope for a presidentially appointed Cabinet and more scope for initiatives from the Presidency.

This did not, however, result in any of the bourgeois weaknesses being overcome. The domestic bourgeoisie's parochial character, its lack of resources, its minimal cultural development (locking most of their main parties into specific religious and ethno-cultural outlooks) resulted in an inability to maintain coalitions as well as a rivalry over access to commercial privileges through bureaucratically issued licences and other state-connected deals. This, in turn, resulted in constant changes of government, of Cabinet composition and, often, of policies. Corruption had, naturally, become endemic. Sukarno began to critique this situation quite early, and suggested that different political parties be 'buried' so that a single political organization, based on the old axis between the radicalized intelligentsia and the mobilized masses, could come into being.

Features of the Guided Democracy Landscape

Though this idea did not meet with popular support, Sukarno was nevertheless able, in 1959, to usher in some changes, the most significant of which was the formation of a new parliament comprising representatives not just from political parties but also from trade unions, peasant groups, etc. Part of the price for this change was, of course, conceding to a representation of the Armed Forces as well, thereby legitimizing their direct involvement in politics.

While this was the main structural change, a number of other decisions and developments were more important in setting up the contours of Guided Democracy and of the trap in which Sukarno and the PKI later found themselves. One was the decision to postpone the general elections due in 1959. Initially, the government had announced that the elections, put off due to financial and administrative reasons, would not be delayed by more than a year. Vigorous protests were voiced by all the parties, including the PKI, who then demanded that the one-year deadline be scrupulously adhered to. These protests must not be interpreted as a step to drastically narrow political representation in the parliament—for the parliament that Sukarno eventually appointed by Presidential decree in 1960 aimed at representation from all political streams, even from banned parties. But it is undeniable that a trend did develop towards abandoning elections which later went on to become a significant (but apparently unrecognized) problem for Sukarno and the PKI.

Another decision—taken in 1960—was the ban on two political parties, the MASYUMI and the PSI. Central leaders of both were involved in the armed insurrections of 1956–58 and in the formation of the PRRI. Both held subsequent congresses during which they refused to repudiate their leaders and their actions. This was construed as support for the armed insurrection and hence sufficient reason for the ban.

Yet another desicion was the declaration of Martial Law at the time of the 1956–58 PRRI rightist rebellions. Martial Law had not ushered in widespread repression, focused as it was on dealing with the military conflicts. However, it did increase the role of the military in the political arena—military officers slowly became part of local executive boards, operating in tandem with provincial administrations. Further, it enabled the Armed Forces to seize managerial control of all those Dutch enterprises which had been nationalized between 1956 and 1958, in the wake of worker occupations under the Left leadership.[20] These enterprises represented the overwhelming majority of the modern sector of Indonesia's economy. Now under military management, they became a major source of corruption and deepened the ties between Army officers and civilian capitalists. Martial Law remained in place until 1962, and the spectre of military repression could only have been enhanced by this as well as by the new representation of the military in parliament.

The primary feature of the Guided Democracy landscape was, however, the rapid increase of mass mobilization which Sukarno considered necessary for strengthening the popular classes against those elements in Indonesian society that were aligned with Western (imperialist) interests. It was also meant to help reorganize political life in such a way as to end the constant factionalism inherent in the domestic bourgeoisie. There is little doubt that Sukarno hoped that the mass campaigns would help build a single, national, political organization based on a fusion of radical intellectuals and radicalized masses. Almost all the campaigns were organized through the National Front, an alliance of all the 10 parties that continued to operate, including the PKI.

The mood of mass mobilization also allowed room for campaigns outside the National Front framework, a fact taken advantage of by both the PKI and the PNI. The most significant National Front campaigns were against continuing Dutch colonialism on West Papua and the integration of West Papua into Indonesia, and, later, against the formation of Malaysia as well as against American cultural influences. Some were also directed towards the nationalization of American, British and Belgian companies. Causes campaigned for by the PKI included worker representation in the management of state companies, land reform and the redistribution of land to landless farmers, wage increases and price control. Both the PKI and PNI also campaigned to disseminate modern culture and the arts among the masses (although in this, especially on matters of sex and gender, they were greatly influenced by the cultural norms of the 1950s and 60s and by Stalinist ideas).[21]

Sukarno regarded mass mobilization as the key to changing Indonesian society and making possible a transformation in the direction of socialism. Mass action as a means of awakening the peasants and workers from the stupor of colonial rule was one of two fundamental concepts for his idea of revolution. The other was internationalism—the need for a worldwide revolution. As he explained in a 1957 speech, he saw his politics more in tune with Trotsky than with Stalin (although he clearly misunderstood Trotsky's theory of permanent revolution).[22]

It was the combination of these campaigns that facilitated the growth of the PKI and the PNI. Their mass organizations recruited millions of members over a span of just two or three years, with the PKI growing the fastest. As the movement grew, so did the issue of how it could come to power. Which was, in effect, the same question as: When and how would a confrontation with the Army take place?

THE *RITULING* TRAP

At the outset of Guided Democracy, the PKI had strongly demanded that the government keep to its promise of holding elections within a year. All its major Central Committee resolutions, as well as its other statements on national politics between 1959 and 1963, continued to voice this need. From 1963 onwards, however, the election question receded from its list of interests. A new framework had been brought into being as a result of the decisions of 1959–60 and the speed at which the mass movement was growing.

Sukarno's idea of a single, united mass movement with a socialist outlook had been present in his thinking as far back as the 1920s, when he wrote the essay 'Nationalism, Islam and Marxism'.[23] According to him, the basis for unity between non-sectarian Marxists, progressive Left nationalists and Muslims was an opposition to imperialism and to class economic exploitation as defined in relation to the extraction of surplus labour (which he interpreted as *riba*, i.e. interest and other unearned income under Islam). This was articulated as opposition to 'exploitation of nation by nation and exploitation of man by man'. A pamphlet about unity, the essay also set out to split conservative from progressive among both the Muslims and the nationalists. This idea was relaunched in the 1960s through the idea of NASAKOM—the unity of nationalism (*NASionalisme*), religion (*Agama*) and Communism (*KOMunisme*).[24]

Sukarno's insistence on NASAKOM unity in an environment of constant mass mobilization had a number of consequences.

One: it was a revolutionary legitimization for the PKI, excluded from the government since 1948. The NASAKOM concept afforded the same legitimacy to communism as was granted to nationalism and religion. In fact, more, since the nationalist and religious movements were obliged to purge themselves of elements supporting imperialism or class exploitation. Sukarno's campaign for NASAKOM, though, did not immediately end the resistance to PKI participation in the government. Even by September 1965, the PKI headed no significant ministries in the Cabinet. NASAKOM did, however, set a new framework within which the PKI could demand participation. Almost all PKI propaganda, especially after 1963, would call for state institutions to be based on a *berporoskan NASAKOM* (NASAKOM axis).

Two: it set up a dynamic of competition, not for votes but for scales of mobilization. The increased pressure on other major NASAKOM participants, the PNI and the Islamic Nahdatul Ulama party (NU), to mobilize in these campaigns eventually created in them a conservative–radical polarization. By 1965, the PNI had adopted a more radical programme and formally expelled its right-wing leadership and the NU central leadership had split in two. Had Guided Democracy survived until 1966, the National Front would have had a more politically homogeneous membership.

The increasingly radical atmosphere, the absence of any effective and open advocacy of right-wing policies and the legitimization of the PKI by NASAKOM led to the adoption of *rituling*—a new strategy for winning power. *Rituling*, or 'retooling' in English, was the policy of replacing members of state-apparatus personnel, including managers of state-owned companies, who were considered either reactionary or corrupt with more progressive counterparts. This idea of a personnel-replacement programme seems to have originated from the Army whose own personnel dominated an institution called the Committee for Retooling the State Apparatus (Panitia Retooling Aparatur Negara, PARAN), which was supposed to supervise this very same task. During 1961–63, the PKI waged a campaign for the dissolution of PARAN and the formation of a new institution under the direct control of Sukarno and a *berporoskan NASAKOM*–communist leadership. This campaign partially succeeded when PARAN was dissolved and replaced with the Supreme Command for the Retooling of the Apparatus of the Revolution (Kommando Tertinggi Retooling Alat Revolusi, KOTRAR), directly under President Sukarno. However, KOTRAR was never NASAKOMized, i.e. PKI personnel were never part of its leadership. PKI statements and resolutions continuing to demand for KOTRAR to 'be improved so that it truly reflects the national *gotong-royong* with NASAKOM as the axis'.[25]

The apex of achievement aimed for through a NASAKOM retooling was a NASAKOM Cabinet, i.e. an effective introduction into the Cabinet of PKI ministers who would then be allowed to head working ministries. Calls for a NASAKOM Cabinet were frequent during January–August 1965; articles in the newspapers increasingly betrayed an impatience with the lack of progress and Sukarno himself continued to both emphasize its necessity and praise the PKI. In a keynote speech in May 1965, for example, he described the PKI as: 'a tremendous element in the explanation of the revolution'.[26]

The PKI's overall analysis of their retooling strategy is worth relating in some detail. A 1963 report, 'The Indonesian Revolution and the Immediate Tasks of the C.P.I.' included a section entitled 'State Power in Indonesia Today' in which Aidit explains: 'each society has a basis and its corresponding superstructure. The basis of a society is its economic structure or production relations while its superstructure is all institutions of politics, law philosophy etc. The State is the most important element of the Superstructure.' The Report goes on to mention that though the basis of Indonesian society continues to be colonial and feudal, there is, nevertheless, a struggle to resist this economic system. Hence, 'the existence of two forces: the forces of the colonial and semi-feudal system and the forces that are fighting for a national and democratic economy.

These realities also find their reflection in the superstructure, including state power and chiefly, the
cabinet' [emphasis in the original].[27]

The PKI's strategy for power was a strategy to
enter and lead the Cabinet, a strategy top-down in
nature. The general political processes whereby this
would be achieved were also outlined in the Report:

> The state power of the Republic of Indonesia is
> a contradiction between two opposing aspects:
> the first aspect is that which represents the in-
> terests of the people. The second aspect is that
> which represents the peoples' enemies. The first
> aspect is embodied in the progressive attitude
> and policy of President Sukarno which enjoys
> the support of the C.P.I. and other sections of
> the people. The second aspect is embodied in
> the attitude and policy of the rightists and the
> die-hards: they are the old established forces.[28]

The position of each 'aspect of the state' is explained in terms of political developments: 'Today
the popular aspect [. . .] leads the course of political
development in the state power of the Republic of

Indonesia.' The aspect representing the peoples' enemies 'no longer leads the course of developments. However, it is still the *dominant* aspect' [emphasis in the original]. Decisions taken by the government in May 1963 to bring in austerity measures (similar to those proposed by the World Bank in 1962 but rejected at the time) are referred to as evidence of its dominance. 'But in any case,' Aidit sums up, 'the state of the Republic of Indonesia as a whole is now led by the forces which represent the people.'[29]

This particular argument, of the central battle in state power between pro- and anti-populist forces and of the key element within the state being the Cabinet, set the framework for the PKI's tactics from 1963. The mobilization of popular forces played a dual role. One: it secured various economic and political demands, ranging from wage rises and price control to land redistribution, nationalization of foreign companies, foreign policies in support of Vietnam and other national liberation struggles. Two: it created the political atmosphere necessary for the retooling of the state apparatus (including, eventually, the Cabinet) along NASAKOM lines.

It is from this moment that calls for general elections began to fade from the resolutions of the PKI.

This approach of the PKI weakened the link between its mass-action activity and any steps towards coming to power. The one significant constraint faced by the PKI was the existence of the Armed Forces which were ready, at any given moment, to physically remove both it and Sukarno from the scene. Hence, it was impossible for the PKI to openly campaign for a popular insurrection—it would have invited an immediate coup and counter-revolution for which neither the PKI nor Sukarno were prepared. The real core of state power—'the body of armed men', as Marx put it—was still, unfortunately, 'dominated' by what Aidit referred to as the anti-people forces. And though the rapid growth of the PKI and the pro-Sukarno forces between 1960 and 1965 meant a huge new membership, those new members needed more time to be informed and trained for such a confrontation.

Abandoning the possibility of arguing for the elections as a mechanism for governmental change, and unable to openly campaign for a populist insurrection, the PKI was left with retooling as its only option. This strategy, however, had many disadvantages, indeed deep flaws, and greatly diminished the significance of the mass mobilizations that both Sukarno and the PKI were encouraging. The retooling, as was being claimed, would have to be done from above, by Sukarno, by KOTRAR, 'legalized' by Presidential or KOTRAR decision. Of course, it is possible to imagine a retooling process carried out directly by the masses, storming offices and kicking out rightist or corrupt officials (as the Indonesian workers had done in 1956–57 in the Dutch enterprises). I have spoken to PKI activists, survivors of 1965, who told me that such a process was what they imagined would eventually happen, although in the 1960s it was not unpopular Dutch expatriates that would have to be removed but Army officers and their cronies.

Rituling's Fundamental Flaws

This strategy for a top-down retooling, especially of the Cabinet, did not help avoid the issue of a confrontation with the Army. While Sukarno was President and head of KOTRAR, with formal powers to retool and appoint a Cabinet, he enjoyed only a minority support from the Armed Forces leadership. Any move by him to bring the PKI into the Cabinet in a way that substantially increased its influence, or to establish an actual Sukarno–PKI radical Left government, would drastically bring forward the dreaded confrontation. As late as September 1965, there was still no openly PKI leader in control of any politically significant ministry.

Also, a major blind spot in this analysis of the state was that it imagined the Cabinet, rather than the state's repressive wing, as its core element. The PKI was unable to seriously campaign for the NASAKOMization of the Armed Forces. In fact, its recognition of the Army's hostility ran so deep that its daily newspaper, *Harian Rakyat* (People's Daily) hardly reported on or provided any analysis, let alone criticism, of its actions, even as late as 1964–65. Instead, from time to time, it would print slogans in support of the Army. Despite being Supreme Commander of the Armed Forces, Sukarno could not, without risking a coup, attempt a radical re-structuring of the officer corps.

It was this very question—of how to NASAKOM the officer corps, i.e. have communist Army officers—that led to the establishment of Aidit's Special Bureau. Set up to secretly recruit Army officers into the PKI, it was deployed on 30 September 1965. Sjam, the Special Bureau head, reported in mid-1965 that, between 1962 and 1964, it had recruited one-third of the corps. The numbers were probably far fewer in reality. The recruitment being secret, the officers were unable to openly politicize other officers and soldiers under their command nor prepare them to defy the majority of conservative officers.

Perhaps the most serious flaw of the retooling approach was its undemocratic character—it neither made use of the gains of bourgeois democracy, such as the electoral process, nor was it able to properly deploy the mobilization of the masses for a democratic insurrection. In fact, retooling caused the PKI to be labelled an undemocratic organization and introduced a fundamental contradiction into its—and Sukarno's—political practice. There was a deeply democratic character to the mass mobilizations of this period, with millions of people being drawn into political activity, discussions and education. The democratic contact between political leaderships, students, intellectuals and the masses was deepened, as evidenced by the rich socialist literature that flourished in this period.[30] The growth in activity of trade unions, peasants' and women's organizations as well as the cultural sphere all testify to this. However, retooling under the pressure of mobilizations, combined with complicated manoeuvrings at higher levels of government, did not always reflect the popular will; indeed, at some times and in some places it most emphatically did not. Pro-PKI district heads, even governors, for example, were appointed in areas with a clear non-PKI majority.[31]

Why did the PKI abandon its support for elections? Its alliance with Sukarno and its support for Guided Democracy may have been one factor. Sukarno had spoken against the system of liberal democracy where 50 per cent plus 1 reigned supreme. His idea of having sectoral groups—workers, farmers, students, writers and so on—directly represented in parliament also posed problems for an election-based system. However, both the 1945 Constitution and its insistence on the inclusion of a gamut of protections for human and democratic rights was accepted by Sukarno's prime minister, Djuanda, as soon as they were presented. The 1945 Constitution also promised elections. There was no necessary contradiction between Guided Democracy and the electoral process: in 1962–63, a Sukarno–PKI–PNI alliance would have easily won and thus legitimized its majority (although this would not have solved the problem of Army hostility).

The Left deprived itself and the masses of the gains of bourgeois democracy when it accepted the banning of MASYUMI and the PSI in 1961, a ban supported by the PKI and which also removed from the scene other important parties opposed to Sukarno. The PKI therefore made the elections appear somewhat redundant as it continued to demand the banning or marginalization of the Right at the same time as it attempted to institutionalize, through administrative means, the Sukarno–PKI (probable) majority. The 'Thesis on the 44th Anniversary of the Communist Party of Indonesia'[32] sums up this approach:

> After the dissolution of the reactionary parties, the Masjumi (Moslem) and the PSI (right-wing socialist), and that there are only ten parties left which all accept the Manipol,[33] it is the duty of all democratic parties to purge themselves of reactionary elements, to prevent the emergence of neo-Masyumism or neo-soskaism,[34] and to guide Manipolist co-operation as well as possible, to guide national gotong-royong with

NASAKOM as the axis and to consistently
resist all manifestations of NASAKOM-phobia,
National Front-phobia, worker-phobia, Com-
munist-phobia.

Not surprisingly, the PKI also called for the
banning of the anti-communist nationalist party
Murba and of the MASYUMI-linked Islamic Students Association (Himpunan Mahasiswa Indonesia, HMI). There is no doubt about the conservative
nature of these groups; they had also cooperated
with the PRRI militarists and later became key con-
tributors to the support base of the Suharto dictatorship. Any leftist or progressive movement in
Indonesia would have naturally campaigned against
them. The formal bans against them, however,
proved counter-productive in the end. Although
these groups were forced into a semi-underground
existence, the government did not seriously curtail
activities; hence their publications, their student
groups and so on continued functioning. These bans
did nothing more than deprive the growing
Sukarno–PKI movement of any mechanism for

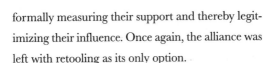

formally measuring their support and thereby legitimizing their influence. Once again, the alliance was left with retooling as its only option.

Rituling, Elections and a Confrontation with the Army

The confrontation between the mobilized popular classes and their opponents—reactionary forces led by the Army—appeared more and more inevitable. The NASAKOM retooling strategy, however, limited the role of the masses to preparing the atmosphere for manoeuvres dictated from above. In the pre-revolutionary situation that developed so rapidly between 1960 and 1965, the most threatening, effective and politically unassailable demand that the mass movement could have mobilized for was the holding of elections. A mass campaign for elections and then an electoral victory would have been highly beneficial to the Left. Such a campaign would not have avoided a confrontation with the military, nor even a coup attempt by the Army leadership, but millions of members of the Left's organizations and

supporters of Sukarno and/or the PKI would have
been prepared to fight back from a political and
moral high ground. But this was not to be for either
the PKI or Sukarno in 1965.

By 1964, the lines had been drawn. NASAKOM:
yes or no. A NASAKOM Cabinet: yes or no. The
abrupt, unplanned and premature crash of the Left
in October 1965 and the complete reversal of all the
processes of the time make it difficult to perceive
Sukarno's thoughts on overcoming the Army's resistance to a socialist Indonesia. There are two
events, however, of which we must make note. One:
the effort to establish an effective (i.e. free from se-
vere internal contradictions) National Front that
could dominate legal and political activity. A major
step in that direction was the Bogor Declaration,
signed in December 1964 by all 10 legal parties after
a long discussion chaired by Sukarno. The 10 parties
reaffirmed their support for the Manipol and for
Sukarno's leadership and pledged not to 'interpret
each others' ideologies in a way meant to cause
damage'. The last being, in essence, a ban on anti-

communist propaganda that may be resorted to by any of the other parties. More progress was made when the PNI purged itself of its right wing and the NU split, for and against Sukarno. However, as noted earlier, this only sent the whole range of purged forces into a semi-underground state, where they increasingly aligned with each other and plotted with the majority anti-communist wing of the Army. Perhaps Sukarno imagined that an overwhelming dominance by a genuinely united National Front, accompanied by high levels of mass mobilization and participation, would be an adequate defence in a stand-off with the Army. It was also in the aftermath of the Bogor Declaration that some in the Sukarno Cabinet moved to have parliament vote for Sukarno as President for Life.

There was, however, another development in 1965 which seemed to point to an awareness on both Sukarno and the PKI's part that even a full 'NASAKOM unity' among the political parties, despite high levels of mobilization in campaigns around socio-economic and political issues as well

as NASAKOMization, may not be enough to with-
stand the Army. In early 1965, after an offer of a
large supply of arms from the People's Republic of
China, Sukarno proposed the formation of a Fifth
Armed Force, an addition to the current Army,
Navy, Air Force and Police. The idea met with quick
support from the PKI and was justified in public as
a force not counter to the Army but necessary in
extraordinary cases such as a sudden British attack.
This particular threat was mentioned because
Indonesian forces were then assisting guerrillas in
Sabah and Sarawak in their battle against the British.
The justification was flimsy and the Armed Forces
strongly opposed the idea. Talks continued between
Sukarno and the Army leadership. According to the
memoirs of Dr H. Subandrio, the foreign minister
and head of intelligence in 1965, General Ahmad
Yani, commander of the Indonesia Army, had an appointment with the President at 8 a.m. on 1 October
for further discussions on this topic. General Yani was
apparently of the opinion that Sukarno was going to
sack him because of his opposition to the Fifth

Force.[35] As it turned out, he was one of the generals killed in the 30 September Movement, hours before his appointment with Sukarno.

1965: Intensification of the Struggle

April 26: a million people mobilize in Surabaya, Indonesia's second biggest city, in support of the Vietnamese revolution.

10 May: Chairperson of the PNI, Ali Sastroamidjojo, announces support for NASAKOMization 'in all fields'.

24 May: Sukarno praises the PKI at a major rally as a 'major force in explaining the revolution'.

June: large pro-NASAKOM demonstrations.

21 June: The government announces that it recognizes the new government of Algeria, following the coup by leftist Colonel Boumidienne.

25 July: The PKI starts a campaign for the NASAKOMization of Indonesian TV and radio.

29 July: *Harian Rakyat* editorial declares: 'Let's kick out all the false NASAKOMists.'

31 July: A national conference of farmers aligned to the PKI announces it will 'escalate greatly all its revolutionary mass actions'.

7 August: The PNI expels its right-wing leaders.

17 August: *Harian Rakyat* editorial calls for a 'Revolutionary Offensive' to take the revolution to its 'climax'.

19 August: At a huge rally in Jakarta, Sukarno announces the launch of a 'MANIPOL offensive on all fields'. According to *Harian Rakyat*, Sukarno is also ready to announce a decision on the Fifth Force.

20 August: Indonesia leaves the International Monetary Fund and the World Bank.

10 September: *Harian Rakyat* editorial on the urgent need for retooling, especially of the Cabinet.

27 September: *Harian Rakyat* reports on its front page about Aidit urging union activists to not 'just struggle for salted fish, but struggle for *politieke macht* [political power]. [. . .] 'Struggle for a NASAKOM Cabinet with ministers that are known, loved and supported by the people.' It also reports on a speech

by Sukarno beneath the headlines: 'Don't refuse to fulfil the demands of the people!'

Mobilizations increased rapidly during these months, not only for NASAKOMization and re-tooling but also for price control, land distribution and the arrest of corrupt officials.

There was, thus, an increasing sense of things coming to a head. But several issues still needed to be resolved. Would a new, more homogeneous and pro-NASAKOM National Front really emerge? Would a Fifth Force really be established? And how would the Army react? When and how would Sukarno have a majority in the Army? While events were indeed hurtling towards a climax, it is unlikely that even Sukarno had any inkling of it appearing in the shape of the conspiracy of 30 September.

Returning to 30 September

Although Sukarno shrugged off the occasional public warnings about the Army's hostility, there was little doubt that the idea of a Fifth Force appealed to him precisely because of that hostility, manifested over the years through attempted coups, rebellions, insurrections and assassination attempts. The same reason explains why the idea enjoyed the PKI's support. But the proposal for the Fifth Force was more a provocation to the anti-communist majority in the Army than a solution for its hostility.

As popular pressure grew, the PKI appeared to be locked into a position of incremental retooling, including, as already mentioned, the secret recruiting of Army officers. While there are reports that the PKI called for elections in the early part of 1965, there are no signs of any overt public campaign for the same. There are, for example, virtually no mentions of elections in *Harian Rakyat* in 1965. Working to win a majority in the officer corps while continuing to build the mass movement may have seemed the only way forward, although the events after 1965 revealed just how sizeable and consolidated the right wing was in the Army.

Aidit was perhaps searching for a way to demolish the roadblock of Army resistance, beyond that of working in tandem with Sukarno to win over more officers. Throughout August and September, the Special Bureau worked to plan the detention of key generals in the high command and their presentation to Sukarno as disloyal conspirators. According to John Roosa, Aidit had been impressed by Huari Boumedienne's coup in Algeria and its being followed by supportive mass mobilizations. What the Special Bureau planned was not a coup but a military action which then, they hoped, would be supported by mass actions. A conspiracy, the plan aimed at a unilateral retooling of the Army's leadership.

The plan, however, failed at the very start when a few generals, an officer and a child were killed. The anti-communist majority in the Army now had both the opportunity and the pretext to initiate their counter-revolutionary pre-emptive purge. The PKI issued statements to *Harian Rakyat*, supporting the 30 September Movement despite the conspirators calling on the radio for the decommissioning of the Cabinet. The PKI had an impossible case to defend in the face of this botched attempt—made all the worse by the fact that none of its leaders, other than

Aidit and his Special Bureau, had any knowledge of the plan. And both the PKI's and Sukarno's mass support had absolutely no resources to combat the counter-revolution as it slammed into them.

There can be little doubt that aspects of the PKI's alliance with Sukarno were partly responsible for the PKI's plight. This is not to say that the alliance resulted in the moderation of the party's militancy. Indeed as time went on, Sukarno himself moved increasingly to the Left, both on policy issues and in his support for the PKI itself. Whatever Sukarno's contradictions were, he had neither the will nor the power to restrain the PKI or the masses from radicalizing.

The PKI had also, since the 1920s, oriented itself along the international communist movement and looked to the Soviet Union for leadership. By the 1960s, though the PKI maintained links with both Russia and China, its relations with the Communist Party of China (CPC) had grown significantly stronger. The Soviet–China split was, in the 1960s, regarded by supporters of the CPC as a contest between the strategy of protracted peoples' war and that of the parliamentary road to power. A significant factor in the polemics between Moscow and Beijing was that the original Marxist strategy of mass action, codified in the 1920s by the Comintern, had completely disappeared from the agenda. Mass action and insurrection lost out in the contest between the peaceful parliamentary method and armed guerrilla struggle. There was thus little discussion in PKI theoretical journals and materials of the nature of mass action and its relationship to the winning of power. In some respects Sukarno was a more persistent agitator for mass action as a political tool than was the PKI. He emphasized, in the 1920s and the 1960s, that *machtsvorming* (the Dutch word for 'power formation') was the primary way to win power, and, as mentioned earlier, it was this emphasis on mass action that led him to identify with Trotsky rather than Stalin.[36]

Mass action as a strategy requires appropriate tactics, in particular an effective identification of the issues around which to mobilize. In Indonesia, in the 1960s, both Sukarno and the PKI had opted for mass-action mobilizations supporting the NASA-KOMization of the Cabinet. Thereby transforming a mass-based strategy into a tactic for a top-down retooling.

The real problem, however, was the PKI's acquiescence with, even encouragement of, the abandonment of the democratic gains of national revolution, especially of the electoral process. This deprived the PKI (and Sukarno) of a political terrain wherein popular support for them and their policies could be democratically tested in a manner which the Army would find difficult to contest on any reasonable grounds. A mass-action based campaign calling for elections, then campaigning for the Left and mobilizing to defend the vote would have created an environment less fertile for conspiratorial solutions. It may not have prevented a coup or other attempts at counter-revolutionary suppression and may perhaps even have required an insurrection, i.e. a revolution, to defend it but it would have also created an atmosphere less open to provocation.

The rapid growth of the Left and the increasingly radical stance of Sukarno, who also withdrew Indonesia from the United Nations in 1965, was of great concern to both Washington and London. Washington had already been involved in two major interventions in Indonesia, politically in 1948 and militarily in 1956–58. In fact, in the 1950s, according to Audrey R. Kahin and George McT. Kahin, the Eisenhower administration had even decided that, if necessary, it would promote the splitting up of Indonesia and the separation of Java—which it regarded as the home base of the Left—from the rest of the country. While the PRRI rebellion was underway, Eisenhower dispatched the 7th fleet to Indonesia but the rebellion was defeated before the US could intervene.[37] By 1964, British and Indonesian troops were in military conflict in Borneo and Indonesian paratroopers made symbolic landings into peninsular Malaysia.

Roosa cites ample evidence of discussion within US, British and allied government diplomatic circles revealing both their increasing hostility to these political developments in Indonesia and the solution they thought most effective: 'From our point of view, of course, an unsuccessful coup attempt by the PKI might be the most effective development to start a reversal of political trends in Indonesia.'[38]

Communication between the US and the Indonesian Army leadership intensified in 1965, with the US assuring the Army of full support in any confrontation with Sukarno and the PKI. The Army leaders in particular were confident of victory: General Yani claimed 'we'll wipe them out'[39] and General Abdul Haris Nasution told Howard P. Jones, US Ambassador in Indonesia, that the Madium fiasco 'would be mild compared with an army crackdown today'. It will not be surprising if one discovers that the US and the UK actually helped create an atmosphere rife with the expectation of an Army coup, all the while hoping that the PKI would act first. However, Jones did not expect the PKI to fall so easily into the trap. In March 1965, in an internal speech in Washington, Jones told State Department officials: 'Unless the PKI Leadership is rasher than

I think they are, they will not give the army the clear-cut kind of challenge which could galvanise effective reaction.'[40] 'Contrary to Jones' expectation [. . .] Aidit and Sjam did walk into the trap.'[41]

Although the prospect of a NASAKOM Cabinet no longer seemed easily attainable, the larger PKI leadership refused to give up and were content with waiting patiently. Jones evidently was of the same mind, for he told his colleagues, in the course of the same speech: 'The PKI is doing too well through its present tactics with Sukarno.'[42]

Why then did Aidit decide to act so rashly?

Perhaps he was overly convinced by the assessments provided by Sjam about the Special Bureau's recruitment successes among the Armed Forces, especially the Navy and Air Force. Perhaps he believed that the entire operation—detaining the officers and presenting them to Sukarno—would be a simple, swift and smooth affair.

In any case, the conspiracy tried and failed. And so it was the 30 September Movement that provided the pretext for the final confrontation with the Army rather than either the installation of a Sukarno-appointed National Front NASAKOM government or a mass campaign for elections.

The Army carried out what General Yani had promised Colonel George Benson of the US Army and US military attaché in Indonesia (1956–60), and what General Nasution had promised Jones: a massacre. The CIA helped by providing some of the names for assassination and arrest. And the course of Indonesian history was reversed for 33 years and the country itself was redefined. It is out of this barren landscape that a new Left emerged in the 1990s. Not surprisingly, it was the efforts of the most courageous and most humanist of the Sukarnoist survivors that provided the bridge between the first radical resentments against the new Indonesia's sterility and corruption and the emergence of new, organized left-wing activists.

INDONESIA'S NEW LEFT

It is difficult to convey the true extent of the social purge that took place after 1965. Terror was the only weapon, and murder and torture its main techniques. A particularly rotten form of black propaganda deepened the fear and hatred in that part of society, often religious, that was already anti-communist. One of the main features of this propaganda was the systematic spreading of the rumour that several of the executed generals had been tortured—in the most sordid and degrading manner—before they were killed, a fact which the Army's own autopsy reports completely refuted. The Catholic newspaper, *KOMPAS*, now the leading daily newspaper in Jakarta, published, for example, descriptions of women dancing naked in front of the captive Generals in a manner reminiscent of cannibalist ceremonies executed by the primitive tribes of earlier centuries.

Shortly after, another daily published the following 'confession':

[. . .] ordered us to hit this person hard; then to stab this person's genitals with the penknives. The first person we saw hitting and stabbing the person's genitals was the leader of Gerwani from Tanjung Priok named S. and Mrs. Sas. Next several other friends [went]. The ones I knew were Si and A who went next. After that, we ourselves joined in torturing that person. All the women, which was not less than 100 people went next and witnessed it. Next we saw the victim brought close to the well by people wearing striped uniforms. . . .

The victim was shot three times, then he fell; but he wasn't dead yet. Someone in a green uniform [. . .] ordered the Gerwani to advance. Everyone did what they had before, stabbing the genitals of the victim, and with the razors, sliced his genitals and body; to the point that he died. At that time, I was asked by friends who the person who had been killed was, said Djamilah, but our mouths instead were struck so that we no longer dared to ask.[43]

This kind of black propaganda was systematically pumped into the press within just three days of the 30 September Movement, and was carried out for months, in one form or the other, alongside the purge. It is likely that the propaganda was particularly strong within the Army in order to justify the terror that it unleashed and as reinforcement for the public display of decapitated heads in villages or the rivers clogged with headless bodies.

Even after its most intense period, vestiges of this propaganda was sustained in many other forms. Textbooks treated it as a fact. An epic feature film was made based on Suharto's version of the events of the 30 September Movement, replete with bloodthirsty, communist women dancing before their victims, generals having their eyes gouged out, bloodletting and screaming.

Then whole new histories were written, not simply of the 30 September Movement but of the entire Indonesian past. Specific aspects were singled out. The treasonous character of the PKI was one. The heroic history of General Suharto—starting from his alleged activity in the revolutionary war in 1945—was another. The erasure of memory took place on a mass scale. Indeed, even the capacity to remember any aspect of social and political experience disappeared altogether as the history taught in the schools was a series of crude lies which the students were expected to learn by rote.

A 60-year-long, rich and humane history of revolt—the entire experience of popular struggle against the Dutch and then against neo-colonialism—was thus wiped away from national memory, and especially from the memory of the popular classes. All physical reminders of the Left were destroyed, and the majority of left-wing political prisoners were moved to the isolated island of Buru in eastern Indonesia and forced to build their camps in the bush. Every single book or article by the Left, including Sukarno's, became impossible to locate. Until he was put under house arrest in 1968, Sukarno continued to speak out against the massacres and in defence of the PKI but none of his statements were revealed to the public.

Indonesian society was denied even a basic introduction to the modestly critical assessment of twentieth-century world history.

How could the Left ever revive? Indeed, even more than 40 years after the worst of the terror and 10 years after the fall of Suharto, the organized Left can still be counted only in the hundreds, at most thousands, in a country of 250 million.

Yet the story is not simple. The political history of Indonesia from 1970 until today, especially until 1998, has been a history of escalating protest and revolt with each passing decade.[44] It has been a history marked by the ability of very small forces, sometimes even a few individuals, to galvanize a popular democratic sentiment—even one that barely survived the times—into an influential political tool.

Between 1973 and 1974, students from the University of Indonesia in Jakarta, Gajah Mada University in Jogjakarta and the Bandung Institute of Technology to name a few organized a wave of protests against corruption, the rich–poor gap and foreign investment and demanded more democratic rights. This sparked an outbreak of mass rioting which *almost* allowed the dictator's rivals within the regime to seize power from him. Almost, for his rivals hesitated and he gripped the reins tighter than before. More than a hundred students and intellectuals were arrested, and detained for terms ranging between one and six years, and sympathetic newspapers were shut down. Only three of the detainees were put on trial and sentenced. Another round of protests occurred in 1978; this time, all forms of political activity on university campuses was banned and more students arrested, tried and imprisoned. The individual who had become the voice of these protests, the poet and dramatist Rendra, was imprisoned for almost a year and without trial.

These protests, and the poetry and imagery created by Rendra, recovered from Suharto's redefinition of Indonesia something of the country's history of struggle and popular democratic ideology. During the 1970s, Rendra wrote many poems and staged several plays which harked back to the spirit

of the earlier struggles. In 'A Poem of an Old Man
Under a Tree', he writes:

> Do you think a fart can replace justice?
> Here human rights are taken away
> To defend the rich and established
> Workers, peasants, fishermen, journalists and
>   students
> Have been made powerless
>
> O, falsehood now idol of all
> How much further can you defy reality

Workers, peasants, fishermen return to the political
stage as the subjects of oppression but not yet as the
agents of change. Nevertheless, Rendra's poems
confronted his audiences—sometimes in the thousands—and his readers with the question of taking
sides. Such as in 'Poem of a Student Meeting':

> Yes!
> There are those triumphant, those who are
>   humiliated
> Those with weapons, those with wounds
> There are those who sit, and those who are sat
>   upon
> Those with abundance, those from who so
>   much has been taken

And we ask here:
'for whom are your good intentions?
On whose side do you stand?'[45]

Rendra was arrested the day after one of his mass poetry readings in Jakarta and spent most of 1978 in prison. A poet and some student councils almost split wide open the dictatorship, exposing Suharto to attack from his rivals. Suharto recovered, however, and tightened his control over even the lowest layer of anti-communist liberals—they were the ones who spoke their minds about popular democratic ideas, who helped mobilize students on the street and created an atmosphere that encouraged the masses to protest and vent their anger.

These students found their mentors in people like Rendra and other intellectuals who had been opponents of Sukarno and the Left before 1965, alienated from the cult status that Sukarno was acquiring and from what seemed to them to be the autocratic retooling exercises. Lacking the ideology to critique Sukarno and the PKI from a leftist perspective, these intellectuals—many from the PSI—initially fell in behind Suharto and his suppression of the Left. By the 1970s they turned against him and began to influence a new generation of students to oppose him at the same time as they instilled in them their anti-Sukarno and anti-PKI sentiments of the 1960s.

By the 1980s, the monopoly of this PSI mentoring declined and political activism began to be imbued with a more explicitly left-wing outlook. This was achieved through the work of just three men: novelist Pramoedya Ananta Toer and journalists Hasyim Rachman and Joesoef Isak, who were among the almost 20,000 leftists imprisoned until the late 1970s. Toer and Rachman had been together for most of their detainment in Buru Island prison camp. Isak had been in Jakarta. In 1980, defying the ban on the involvement of former political prisoners in 'vital industries', they formed the publishing company Hasta Mitra and published Ananta Toer's Buru Quartet: *This Earth of Mankind* (*Bumi Manusiya*, 1980), *Child of All Nations* (*Anak semua bangsa*, 1980), *Footsteps* (*Jejak langkah*, 1985) and *House of Glass* (*Rumah kaca*, 1988). *This Earth of Mankind* in particular caused an enormous furore, as it was authored and published by men associated, according to the regime's propaganda, with those who had tortured and killed the Generals in 1965. It caused even more of a furore when it received critical support in the press. Adam Malik, Suharto's vice-president, the modestly maverick and former 1940s' radical, met the three men and allowed the major newspapers to photograph him with them. He even advocated that the books be read in the schools. Suharto had to wait several months and engineer quite a few protests before *This Earth of Mankind* was banned. Undaunted, Hasta Mitra continued to publish the sequels to this book; each was banned upon its release.

The publication of these books, an impossible feat during the Suharto regime but for the outstanding courage of this trio, had a range of outcomes. First: the humanity and beauty of the novels dispelled the myth that such men were devils. Second: it introduced a whole generation of young people, mainly students, to people from the Left. Varying levels of dialogue with these three men, and other released prisoners, could finally begin. Third: the books punctured the myth that it had been military figures at the vanguard of the struggle—they had been, in reality, writers, journalists and peasants, all motivated by thoughts of humanism and freedom. Fourth: it hinted, effectively, at the link between the first revolutionary democrats and the emergence of the Left by introducing characters whom people recognized as connected to the early Indonesian Communist Party.

The publication of these books, the courage of their content and the tenacity of the publishers—who were repeatedly harassed; Isak was even imprisoned for three months—the dialogue with the released prisoners and the revived interest in Left history were key factors contributing to a new current of political thought among the students that was outside the hegemony of the anti-communist PSI liberals. Study clubs, community development groups and human rights groups began to emerge. By 1989, some student radicals were even helping organize peasant protests and land occupations. The pre-1965 Left, in the form of Hasta Mitra, had sown seeds in the soil made fertile by Rendra and the students of the 1970s.

Student-activist groups forged more and more links with groups of farmers and factory-workers. One such network eventually established the Students in Solidarity with Indonesian Democracy (Solidaritas Mahasiswa Indonesia untuk Demokrasi, SMID) in 1992. The SMID activists in turn established the People's Democratic Party (Partai Rakyat Demokratik, PRD) in 1994, announcing its formation at a meeting attended by Isak, Rachman and Ananta Toer. Between 1994 and 1996, the PRD organized a series of student-worker strikes and protests, demanding the right to organize, wage increases, an end to the role of the military in politics and a repeal of all laws giving the state control over political life. The PRD's campaigns for a return to mass-action politics coincided with a growing unease and frustration among the marginalized sections of the bourgeoisie who began to rally around one of the three political parties 'allowed' by the regime, the Indonesian Democratic Party (Partai Demokrasi Indonesia, PDI), headed by the hitherto silent Megawati Sukarnoputri, one of Sukarno's daughters. The PRD, its militant campaigning facing repeated violent dispersal, and Megawati, stubbornly refusing to surrender leadership of the PDI after it became clear that Suharto wanted her deposed, came together in June–July 1996. Demonstrations of the two forces took place and were immediately put down by the Armed Forces. The regime moved swiftly: it declared Megawati's party illegal, established a puppet PDI and forcibly removed Megawati's supporters from the PDI office. Many PDI members were killed, thus causing more protests and rioting across Jakarta.

The regime, well aware of the PRD's role in popularizing street mobilizations as a method of protest and its role in distributing radical literature, declared it responsible for the rioting and ordered the arrest of all PRD members. Fourteen were captured while the others continued to protest, through new front committees, despite being forced underground.

The populist sentiment was reawakened and, between July 1996 and May 1998, the protest gathered
momentum. It was given an extra boost when the
Asian financial crisis further eroded Suharto's credi-
bility, already repeatedly mauled by corruption scan-
dals and the extravagant lifestyle of his wife and
children. Student protests, backed by widespread
popular sentiment, spread throughout the country
despite increasingly frequent violent dispersals. The
most extreme Suharto men in the military began to
kidnap activists—but it was too late. The protests
were too substantial and militant and now threatened
to radicalize. The Indonesian elite were quick to
abandon Suharto, for they faced the prospect of public fury if they continued to remain loyal to his
regime.

The PRD was never a large party—perhaps at
its height it comprised several hundred members—
with affiliated worker and student organizations of
several thousands. It was not the only protest group
active against Suharto but it was the only one to pro-
vide a clear tactical direction and to base itself on a

leftist perspective of mass action. It was no wonder then, that during its relaunch in 1997, Ananta Toer took the symbolic step of publicly joining the PRD.

The Indonesian bourgeoisie's decision to ditch Suharto in 1998 has won them some stability over the last 10 years. It demobilized a mass movement by conceding its main demand just as the movement was beginning to grow, before any national leaders were established and before any new (revived) ideology could harness the energies of populist sentiment to dispel the barrenness of ideas in Indonesian political life. A new configuration of elite factions, although always jostling over money and position, has enjoyed a stable government for 10 years.

This does not mean that social discontent disappeared. Street protest continued unabated, but now atomized and fragmented, without national leadership and focus. A deep frustration among the masses with all the existing political parties grew evident as participation in elections dropped from 93 per cent in 1999 to just over 50 per cent in 2009. The streets were rife with anger and hatred.

In this situation, the Indonesian new Left took two steps back and three steps forward. Faced with a suddenly demobilized national student movement, the PRD developed internal differences over the way forward. One by one, former leaders from the 1990s crossed over to the mainstream bourgeois parties. In 2007, one leader took a majority of the party in that direction, first supporting a discredited small-centre Islamic party and then dividing its support between Suharto's old party, GOLKAR (Partai Golongan Karya, or the Party of the Functional Groups) and an alliance between Megawati and the General who organized the kidnapping of PRD activists in 1997–98. Another section, now organizing and campaigning under the name of the Political Committee of the Poor People's Democratic Party (Komite Politik Rakyat Miskin–Partai Rakyat Demokratik, KPRM-PRD) is rebuilding and relaunching its campaigns and its publications.

So, 10 years after the fall of Suharto, the KPRM-PRD, as the organized body of the Left since the 1990s, and a concentrated centre of 19 years' experience in radical politics, comprises only a few hundred full-time activists, smaller than it was at its peak in the 1997–2001 period. The split was at least two steps back. Rebuilding has been one, perhaps two, steps forward.

But more has happened. In 1998, when Suharto fell, there was one nationally organized and openly left-wing political organization, sufficiently so for Ananta Toer, Rachman and Isak to identify with it. Of course, there were many other human rights groups, women's rights and labour organziations that were neither ideologically Left nor revolutionary. Ten years after Suharto, the PRD in the form of the KPRM-PRD continues to campaign and to rebuild. In addition, there are now at least three other nationally organized openly socialist or radical groups: the Working Peoples' Association (Perhimpunan Rakyat Rekerjam, PRP), the Indonesian Struggle Centre (Partai Pemuda Indonesia, PPI) and forces that mobilize under the banner of the People's Struggle Front (Front Perjuangan Rakya, FPR). Left and Marxist groups mushroom at the local level and one can observe the presence of many new Left websites. New radical publishers bring out the writing of Indonesia's historical Left as well as all traditions of the international Left. The number of organized Left activists has greatly multiplied in a just a few years and will continue to do so.

This new, post-2000, Left has yet to be fully tested. It is gathering its initial cadre and will struggle over different aspects as a potential basis of unity. The ideological and intellectual component of the struggle will intensify as well as organize on the ground. There is no doubt that understanding Indonesia's Left history and its lessons will be a crucial ingredient in any future ideological process. The last few years have witnessed the deaths of Rachman, Ananta Toer, Isak and Rendra.

An era has passed. And the baton has been handed over.

Notes

1   Robert Cribb and Audrey R. Kahin, *A Historical Dictionary of Indonesia*, 2nd edn (Landham, MD: Scarecrow Press, 2004 [1992]), pp. 264–5. Hereafter, I will refer to this work as *HDI*.

2   See John Hughes, *The End of Sukarno: A Coup That Misfired, A Purge That Ran Wild*, 3rd edn (Singapore: Archipelago Press, 2002 [1968]).

3   *HDI*, pp. 321–3.

4   Ibid., pp. 324–5.

5   See Chapter 2, 'Counter-revolution', in Max Lane, *Unfinished Nation: Indonesia Before and After Suharto* (London: Verso, 2008).

6   See Chapter 4, 'Memory', in ibid.

7   Andre Vltchek and Rossie Indira, *Exile: Conversations with Pramoedya Ananta Toer* (Chicago: Haymarket Books, 2006), p. 102.

8   On Aidit and the Special Bureau, see Chapter 4, 'Sjam and the Special Bureau', in John Roosa, *Pretext for Mass Murder: The 30 September Movement and Suharto's Coup d'Etat in Indonesia* (Madison: University of Wisconsin Press, 2006).

9   This account of the events of 30 September and 1 October draws primarily on Roosa's *Pretext*

for Mass Murder. This is both the most recent and most convincing account of these events to date.

10 Roosa, *Pretext for Mass Murder*, p. 219.

11 Sukarno, 'Imperialism in Indonesia', in Sukarno, *Under the Banner of the Revolution* [*Di Bawah Bendera Revolusi*], VOL. 1 (Jakarta: Panitya Penerbitan, 1966), p. 143.

12 For a detailed but tentative account in English of these unclear events, see Ann Swift, *The Road to Madiun: The Indonesian Communist Uprising of 1948* (Ithaca: Cornell Southeast Asia Program Publications, 1989). For an account stressing the role of the United States pressuring for a confrontation and the complicity of Hatta, see Harsutejo, *G30S, sejarah yang digelapkan: tangan berdarah CIA dan rejim Suharto* [30 September, a Hidden History: the CIA and the Bloody Hands of Suharto's Regime] (Jakarta: Hasta Mitra, 2003).

13 See the early section of Harsutejo, *G30S*.

14 *HDI*, pp. 360–2.

15 Ibid., pp. 262–3. A right-wing party campaigning under an Islamic banner, MASYUMI was one of the country's four biggest parties in the 1955 elections, winning 20.9 per cent of the vote.

16 Ibid., p. 328.

17 Ibid., p. 136.

18 See Donald Hindley, *The Communist Party of In-donesia, 1951–1963* (Berkeley: University of California Press, 1966).

19 *HDI*, pp. 164–5.

20 *HDI*, p. 291.

21 Keith Foulcher, *Social Commitment in Literature and the Arts: the Indonesian 'Institute of People's Culture, 1950–1965'* (Clayton, Victoria: Monash University, 1986); Rhoma Dwi Aria Yuliantri and Muhidin M. Dahlan, *Lekra tak membakar buku: suara senyap lembar kebudayaan* Harian Rakjat, *1950–1965* [*Lekra* Does Not Burn Books: The Silent Voices of the Cultural Pages of the Peoples' Daily Newspaper, 1950–65] (Jogjakarta: Merakesumba, 2008).

22 See NOTE 36.

23 Sukarno, *Nationalism, Islam and Marxism* [*Nasionalisme, Islam dan Marxisme*] (Karel H. Warouw and Peter D. Weldon trans.; Ruth T. McVey introd.) (Ithaca: Cornell University, 1970).

24 *HDI*, pp. 286–7.

25 'Resolutions of the First National Conference of

the C.P.I.', *Review of Indonesia* 8 (1964): 16. *Gotong-royong* means cooperation.

26 *Harian Rakyat* (24 May 1965), p. 1.

27 'The Indonesian Revolution and the Immediate Tasks of the C.P.I.', in Supplement, *Review of Indonesia* 2–4 (1963): 13–15.

28 Ibid., p. 14.

29 Ibid.

30 Yuliantri and Dahlan, *Lekra tak membakar buku* and Foulcher, *Social Commitment in Literature and the Arts.*

31 The most famous case would have been in Bali where he appointed Suteja, a pro-PKI figure, despite the PNI being the majority party.

32 'Thesis on the 44th Anniversary of the Communist Party of Indonesia', *Review of Indonesia* 7 (July 1964): 15–16.

33 *Manifesto Politik*: a manifesto which, in very broad terms, called for support for the 1945 Constitution, Indonesian Socialism, Guided Democracy, Guided Economy and an Indonesian Character.

34 *Sos-ka—sosialisme kanan* or right-wing socialism.

35 H. Subandrio, *Yang saya alami peristiwa G30S: Sebelum, saat meletus dan sesudahnya* [My Experiences

of the 30th September Movement Incident: Before, During and After] (Jakarta: Bumi Intitama Sejahtera, 2006). Subandrio spent 30 years in prison after a death sentence was commuted (after, according to him, written pleas from Lyndon Johnson and Queen Elizabeth II).

36 Sukarno outlines his comparison between Stalin and Trotsky in a 1956 speech on 'humanism' or internationalism. The speech has recently been republished in Sukarno, *Bung Karno—Menggali Pancasila—Kumpulan Pidato* [Bung Karno—Excavating Pancasila—Selected Speeches] (Jakarta: Gramedia, 2001), pp. 206–11. Sukarno interprets 'permanent revolution' as the reason for ongoing mass mobilization so that, having conquered governmental power, the revolutionary process may be taken into new social arenas.

37 Audrey R. Kahin and George McT. Kahin, *Subversion as Foreign Policy: The Secret Eisenhower and Dulles Debacle in Indonesia* (New York: New Press, 1995).

38 Howard P. Jones, United States Ambassador to Indonesia, March 1965. Quoted in Roosa, *Pretext for Mass Murder*, p. 176.

39 Ibid., p. 192.

40 Ibid., p. 193.

41 Ibid.

42 Ibid.

43 Charlie Sullivan, 'Sacred Mother or Commie Whore: Images of Indonesian Women at the Birth of the New Order, 1965'. Unpublished paper; course material at University of Michigan, Ann Abor, 2008. Quotes from *Kompas* (10 November 1965, p. 3), and *Api Pancasila* (11 June 1966, p. 2) as translated and cited by Sullivan.

44 See Lane, *Unfinished Nation* for a history of this process. For a liberal academic account, see Edward Aspinall, *Opposing Suharto: Compromise, Resistance, and Regime Change in Indonesia* (Palo Alto, CA: Stanford University Press, 2005).

45 W. S. Rendra, 'Sajak Seorang Tua Dibawah Pohon' ['A Poem of An Old Man Under a Tree'] and 'Sajak Pertemuan Mahasiswa' ['Poem of a Student Meeting'], in *Potret pembangunan dalam puisi* (Jakarta: Lembaga Studi Pembangunan), pp. 102–04 and 50–1, respectively. Both translations are mine.